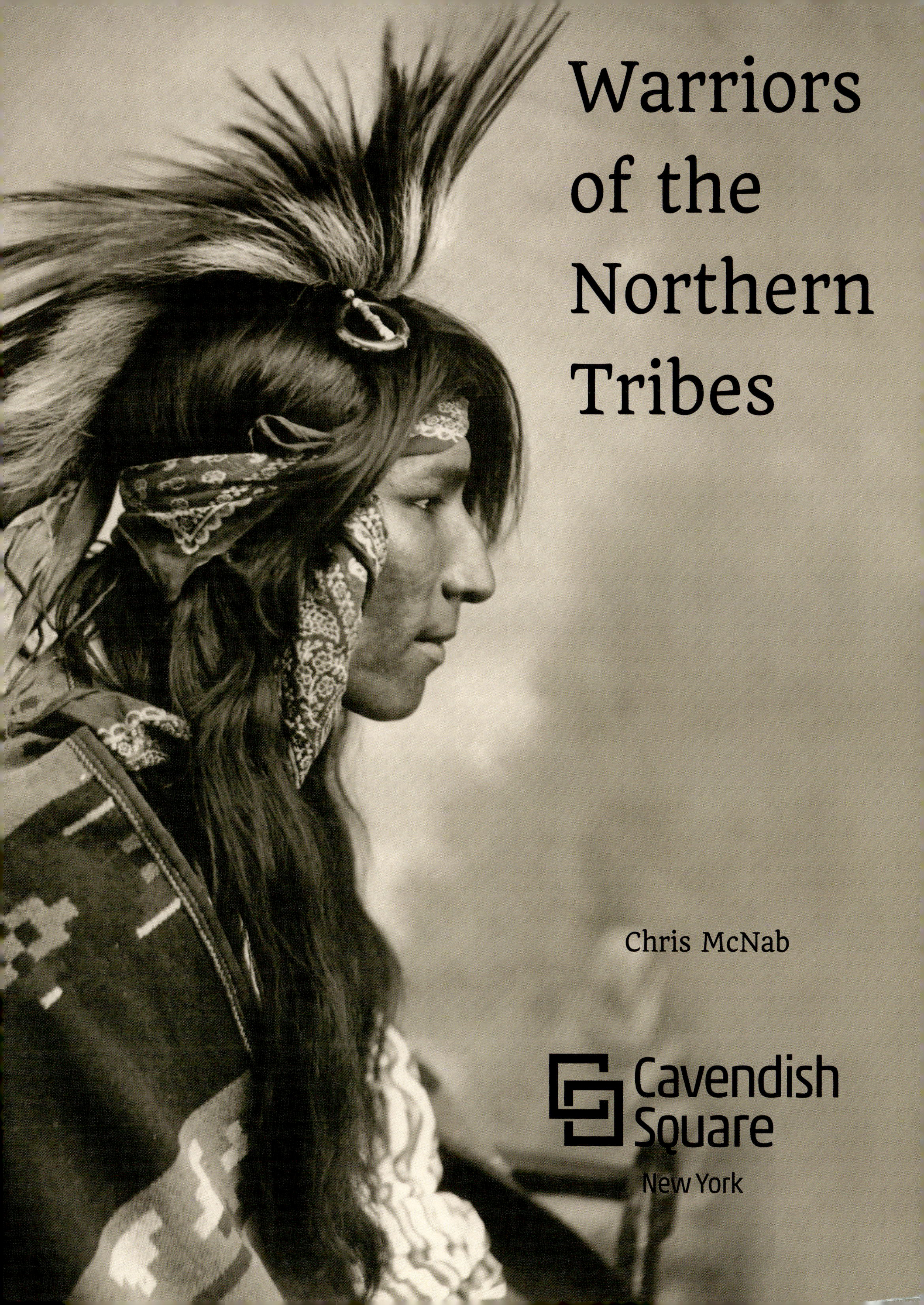

# Warriors of the Northern Tribes

Chris McNab

Cavendish Square
New York

This edition published in 2018 by Cavendish Square Publishing, LLC
243 5th Avenue, Suite 136, New York, NY 10016



First Edition



**Cataloging-in-Publication Data**

Names: McNab, Chris.
Title: Warriors of the northern tribes / Chris McNab.
Description: New York : Cavendish Square, 2018. | Series: Native American warfare | Includes glossary and index. | Audience: Grades 6–10.
Identifiers: ISBN 9781502632852 (library bound) | ISBN 9781502633132 (ebook)
Subjects: LCSH: Indians of North America—Northwest Coast of North America—Juvenile literature. | Indians of North America—Northwest Coast of North America—History—Juvenile literature. | Indians of North America—Canada, Northern—Juvenile literature.
Classification: LCC E78.N78 M37 2018 | DDC 978.004'97—dc23

Editorial Director: David McNamara
Editor: Bernadette Davis
Associate Art Director: Amy Greenan
Production Coordinator: Karol Szymczuk

The photographs in this book are used by permission and through the courtesy of: All maps and black-and-white line artworks produced by JB Illustrations © Amber Books; AKG Images: 47 & 75 (North Wind Picture Archives), 162 (North Wind Picture Archives); Alamy: 98tr (North Wind Picture Archives); Art Archive: 128/129 (William E. Weiss/Buffalo Bill Historical Center), 194 (Buffalo Bill Historical Center); Bridgeman Art Library: 88/89 (Peter Newark American Pictures), 104/105bl (Peter Newark American Pictures), 120 (Look & Learn), 133 (Peter Newark American Pictures), 135 & 151 (Look & Learn), 174 & 197 (Peter Newark American Pictures); Corbis: 19 & 20 (Bettmann), 22t (Werner Forman Archive), 32 (Robert Wagenhoffer), 39 (Marilyn Angel Wynn/Nativestock Pictures), 42, 55 (Medford Historical Society Collection), 56/57 (Historical Picture Archive), 58 (Historical Picture Archive), 62 (Nik Wheeler), 63, 64, 83 (Bettmann), 86 (Peter Harholdt), 112, 137, 143, 146, 152, 157, 158, 159, 160 (Bettmann), 161 (Poodles Rock), 165tr, 165b (Tria Giovan), 176, 184 (Bettmann), 192 (Werner Forman Archive), 206, 209, 210, 211, 214/215 (Bettmann) Dorling Kindersley: 105t (Geoff Brightling) Getty Images: 8 (Bridgeman Art Library), 11 (Roger Viollet), 15 (Joe Sohm/Visions of America), 25 (Time & Life Pictures), 29 (Marilyn Angel Wynn/Nativestock Pictures), 36, 48 & 74 (Bridgeman Art Library), 78br (Science & Society Picture Library), 79tr & 97 (Hulton Archive), 140 & 145 (Time & Life Pictures), 148 (SuperStock), 150 (Bridgeman Art Library), 170/171 (Hulton Archive), 177 (Hulton Archive), 178 (Marilyn Angel Wynn/Nativestock Pictures), 193 (Bridgeman Art Library), 204/205, 207 (Hulton Archive); iStockphoto: 153 (Duncan Walker); Library of Congress: 9, 12/13, 17, 27tr, 41, 45, 49, 50/51, 54, 59, 65tl, 65b, 70, 72tr, 76, 85tl, 85br, 98bl, 100, 106, 109tl, 111, 115, 117, 118, 119, 121, 125, 127tr, 130, 139, 141 (both), 144, 154/155, 156, 163, 164, 167, 168 & 169 (all), 180 (both), 183 & 183 (both), 185, 187, 188, 195, 198/199, 200, 208; Mary Evans Picture Library: 81, 147, 181; Photos.com: 78/79tl, 90, 91, 109b, 127b, 172, 175; Photoshot: 6/7 (World Illustrated), 22bl & 113 (UPPA), 179 (UPPA); Public Domain: 72bl, 122; TopFoto: 102/103 (Granger Collection), 138 & 191 (Granger Collection); U.S. Department of Defense: 213; Werner Forman Archive: 27b (Ohio State Museum), 202 (Anthropological Museum of Lomonosov, Moscow).

Printed in the United States of America

# CONTENTS

Introduction 4

Chapter 1
Tribes of the North 8

Chapter 2
Blackfoot Raiders 16

Chapter 3
From Bows to Firearms 25

Chapter 4
Riel's Rebellions 32

Chapter 5
Arctic and Subarctic Warriors 35

Glossary 44
Further Reading 45
Index 47

# INTRODUCTION

**The tribes of the northern United States and Canada occupied territories ranging from lush plains through to Arctic tundra. Those Native Americans in the northern extremes often managed to preserve their way of life longer than the Native Americans of the east or south, but eventually the depredations of the settlers caught up with them.**

It is evident from surviving eighteenth- and nineteenth-century American literature that the Native Americans living in Canada were often viewed with the same disdain and horror as Native American tribes living elsewhere in North America. The following passage of text comes from an encyclopedia entitled *The Youth's Companion*, compiled and written by Ezra Sampson in 1813, which leaves the reader under no illusions about his impression of the Native Americans north of the Canadian border:

"Canada Indians, tribes as fierce and warlike as any of the aborigines of North America. During a great part of the time that Canada was a province of the French government, which was from its first settlement till its conquest by the British in 1759, the frontiers of the colonies of New-York, Massachusetts and New-Hampshire, were frequently infested by those savages. In the depth of winter, 1689, a party of those Indians, together with a number of Frenchmen, surprized the town of

**◀ Fort McKenzie, August 28, 1833. A group of Assiniboine and Cree indians attack a Blackfoot encampment. The weapons are a mix of the traditional and the modern, with spears and short bows used alongside flintlock muskets.**

Schenectady, in the night, while the inhabitants were unalarmed and in a profound sleep; and butchered them, with circumstances of most horrible barbarity. The whole village was instantly in a blaze; women with child were ripped open, and their infants cast into the flames. Sixty persons perished in the massacre, and twenty-seven were carried into captivity, the rest fled naked through the snow to Albany."

– *Ezra Sampson* (1813)

Making no concessions to his young readership, Sampson goes on in a similar vein for the entire entry, making garish descriptions of children having "their brains beat out against the trees" and women being disembowelled. Yet as with so many colonial sketches of the Native Americans, Sampson is keen to emphasize the horrors at the expense of the more sophisticated aspects of Canadian Native American culture, and their techniques of waging war.

The geographical reach of this resource is extensive, focusing on the Plains Native Americans, a "culture area" that did itself extend into eastern and central Canada. Tribes such as the Cree and Blackfoot, for example, are generally classed as Plains Indians, but they will also be studied in this chapter, not only for their influence on northern North America, but also because their territories embraced a wide spectrum of terrain, including Canadian

**▲ An Assiniboine village, consisting of loosely gathered tipis. Scalps hang from wooden frames outside, signifying earlier victories and declaring the bravery and martial talents of the tipi occupants. Note also the carrying frame attached to the dog in the foreground, which was used to carry weapons as well as supplies on long-distance raids.**

▲ **A Chippewa chief, seen wearing decorative sashes over his tasselled buckskin shirt and a string of wampum beads. The Chippewa were steadily displaced from their lands during the eighteenth and nineteenth centuries.**

mountains and forests. The physical landscape of this region, as we shall see, had a key impact on the type of warfare practised by the indigenous inhabitants.

In the massive Canadian forests, for example, we see styles of warfare similar to those exhibited by the Woodland tribes of the east. Moving further north into the subarctic, however, the severe restrictions of climate and terrain shaped a much more localized and temporary style of conflict, on account of the environment being just as dangerous as any human enemy.

CHAPTER 1

# TRIBES OF THE NORTH

The term "Northern Tribes" covers a large range of tribal territories and peoples. Note that when describing the Native Americans of Canada, excluding the Inuit and the Métis—descendants of marriages between Native Americans and European settlers—it is more correct to refer to the "First Nations," a term that covers all aboriginal peoples in Canada stretching back to the Stone Age. As we are including Alaska in this chapter, however, we will use "Northern" to refer to all Native American people around and north of the Canadian border. They included the Algonquin, Nipissing, Montagnais and Naskapi north of the Great Lakes and up to the Hudson Bay region; the Cree, Chippewa and Algonquin dominating Canada's central regions; the Blackfoot, Ojibway and Assiniboine straddling the Canadian–US border; and the Inuit and Yellowknife occupying the subarctic northern extremes.

In the period covered by this book (1500–1890), the most profound challenge to most of these Northern tribes was the same as that of the US tribes—contact with the colonizing Europeans. During the sixteenth century, both the French and the British made regular visits to Canada's eastern shorelines, their appetites whetted by excellent fishing

**CHIPPEWA NATIVE AMERICAN**
A Chippewa Native American chief, here seen armed with a simple war club, carved from a single piece of wood, and a long spear. The long and well-crafted metal spearhead indicates a post-contact time. Before contact with the settlers and the introduction of metals, the Native Americans tended to tip their spears either through a basic process of fire-hardening, or through the manufacture of chipped flint spearheads.

and the ability to trade European goods with the Native Americans in return for high-quality furs (particularly beaver).

Yet while the British focused most of their colonial muscle on what is today the eastern seaboard of the United States, it was the French who became the dominant foreign settlers in Canada. By the early decades of the seventeenth century, "New France" was beginning to take shape, spurred by Samuel de Champlain's foundation of the city of Québec in 1608. Champlain knew that the fragility of the French colonies in a hostile wilderness necessitated making alliances with the local Native Americans. On this basis, he allied himself with the Algonquin, Huron and Montagnais against the Iroquois, and these tribes would also later assist the French in fighting British expansion.

### Canada and Alaska: Tribal Areas

**The map here shows the major tribal territories of Canada and Alaska, at least in terms of the traditional tribal areas before the displacements caused by settler expansion. The fortunes of the tribes varied according to their geographical location and also their relations with the settlers. No tribal area was entirely free from settler interference. The tribes of subarctic Canada, for example, came into contact with traders for the Hudson's Bay Company during the 1670s, and suffered a consequent loss of major fur resources to the Europeans. Alaskan Native Americans encountered not only settlers pushing up from the south, but also, for a time, Russian traders coming into North America across the Bering Strait.**

**Huron**
A statue of a Huron-Algonquin Native American from explorer Samuel de Champlain's group overlooks the Ottawa River. He carries a quiver of arrows on his back. The French had a variable relationship with the Native Americans they encountered.

### The Beaver Wars

The influx of European colonists, therefore, brought broader hostility between tribes, not just between tribes and settlers. A particularly bitter outpouring of this dissension was the so-called Beaver Wars (1635–84). Trade in beaver furs was a major source of income for the Iroquois and neighboring Huron. Yet such was the demand for furs from Europe that by the 1630s the supply of these animals in the eastern parts of North America was starting to dry up. Yet around the Great Lakes, controlled by the French and the allied Huron, the beaver had managed to maintain its population levels.

The result was war between the Iroquois and the Huron, as the former attempted to move in on the latter's beaver grounds, burning Huron villages and killing both Huron and French citizens. A major Iroquois invasion of Huron territory, 1000 warriors strong, in March 1649 resulted in the destruction of the towns of St. Ignace and St. Louis, near modern Toronto, and the mass exodus of Huron Native Americans from their homelands. Sensing their own power, the Iroquois then attacked other tribes in the Great Lakes region, their war parties sometimes rising to nearly 2000 warriors, before spreading down the Ohio Valley, eventually

▲ **"They See A Lightening Flash And Hear A Roar." Samuel de Champlain (1567–1635) defeats a group of Iroquois with the help of the Algonquins, 1609. The Indians would soon become accustomed to firepower.**

commanding territories from the Ottawa River to Kentucky. As with so many Native American wars, however, success in battle did not bring victory in the overall war. During the 1680s, various tribes, with French assistance, began to claw back their territories around the western Great Lakes and east of the Mississippi. In the Canadian territories, the Chippewa pushed back the Iroquois from around Lake Ontario, and the Iroquois were forced to retreat and finally admit defeat.

Even as the Iroquois were attempting to enforce their monopoly over the fur trade, New France was expanding and consolidating itself, albeit while increasing the friction between French and British imperial interests. At its height in the early eighteenth century, New France stretched from Newfoundland to the Rocky Mountains and from Hudson Bay to the Gulf of Mexico.

Its northern possessions were divided into four main regions; Canada, Acadia, Hudson Bay and Newfoundland (Plaisance). The colonial map changed with the French and Indian War of 1754–63, part of the globally engulfing Seven Years' War (1756–63) between the British and French empires.

The British won out eventually, and from 1764 to 1867, Canada remained under British imperial control

▲ Two Native Americans and three settlers paddle a canoe on Lake George, New York, during the French and Indian War. Native American guides and scouts were essential to the settlers in an unfamiliar landscape.

◀ **An Inuit Indian family cross a river in a traditional Native American canoe. Birchbark canoes could reach up to 24 feet (7.3m) in length.**

▼ **A Native American canoe under construction. The skeleton frame of the canoe was usually made from a wood such as cedar, which was then covered with birchbark panels.**

(borders between Canada and the United States were first formally established in 1783 following the American Revolution), although their rights of possession were tested by conflicts such as the War of 1812 and a series of rebellions in Canada.

### The Cree

It is little wonder, given the state of frequent conflict in North America, that the Northern tribes found themselves struggling for survival. One of the largest tribes in terms of numbers and territorial extent was the Cree, who at their greatest reach had homelands stretching from the Northwest territories down to the plains of Montana. The Cree came into contact with Europeans during the early 1600s, and saw the opportunity to make profitable trade connections with both the French and the British. The way of war amongst the Northern Cree prior to contact with the settlers was similar to that of the Eastern Native Americans. Conflicts consisted of short-lived ambushes and raiding parties designed to acquire patches of territory, settle scores or demonstrate warrior prowess.

The nomadic lifestyle of the Cree, moving camp according to season and hunting ground, meant that more sustained warfare was neither feasible nor relevant. Cree lived in tipis made of birch bark, pine branches and caribou hides, and they could move

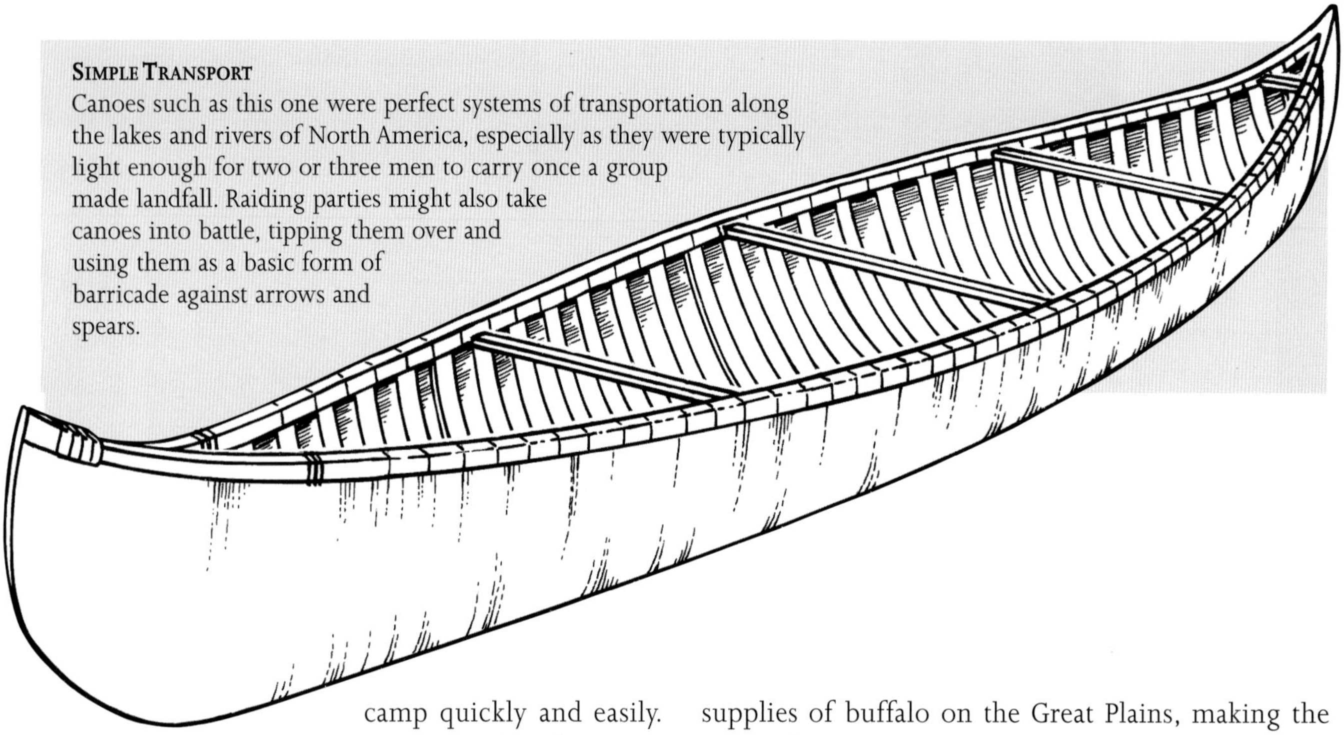

**Simple Transport**
Canoes such as this one were perfect systems of transportation along the lakes and rivers of North America, especially as they were typically light enough for two or three men to carry once a group made landfall. Raiding parties might also take canoes into battle, tipping them over and using them as a basic form of barricade against arrows and spears.

camp quickly and easily.

Among the Cree, therefore, we generally do not see the drive to create fortifications that we saw in the case of the Eastern tribes, although there are other examples of tribal palisade fortifications around the northern edges of the Great Lakes.

Cree males spent much of their time hunting game such as ducks, geese, moose, caribou, deer, beaver and hare, and the act of hunting was accompanied by much ritual and magic related to forest and animal spirits. This magic side to hunting later withered somewhat when the Cree moved further south and discovered seemingly endless supplies of buffalo on the Great Plains, making the spirits far less important in the acquisition of food and hides.

They could move with ease through the wilderness regardless of the season, using snowshoes in the winter and navigating the Canadian rivers in birch bark canoes. Their intimate knowledge of the flora, fauna and landscape meant that the Cree were natural choices for guides and trappers for the British and French settlers. In particular, their interaction with settlers around the Hudson Bay area, a hub of transatlantic trade, meant that in return, the Cree received firearms, a new technology that changed their way of fighting forever.

**TIPI CONSTRUCTION**

Ten to 20 poles made up the frame of a typical tipi, the poles being lashed at the top and positioned precisely on the ground at the bottom to map out the floor area. Bison or deer skins, or panels of canvas, formed the outer covering and were held in place by ropes and pegs attached to the wooden frame. An outlet for smoke was left at the top.

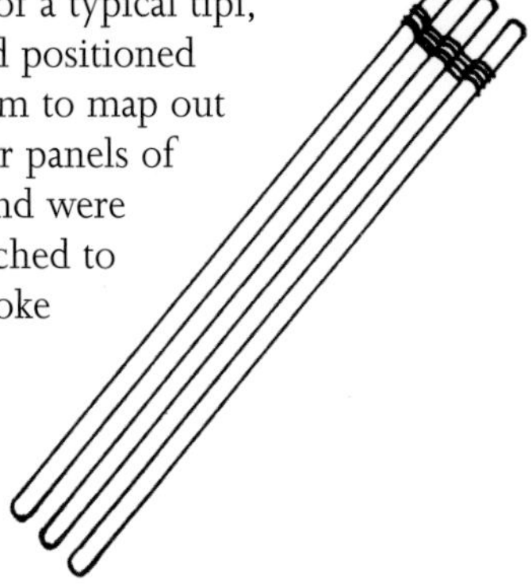

**INSIDE A TIPI**

Life inside a tipi was warm and communal. These habitations were vulnerable to attack, however, especially to arrows or firearms fired through smoke or entrance flaps.

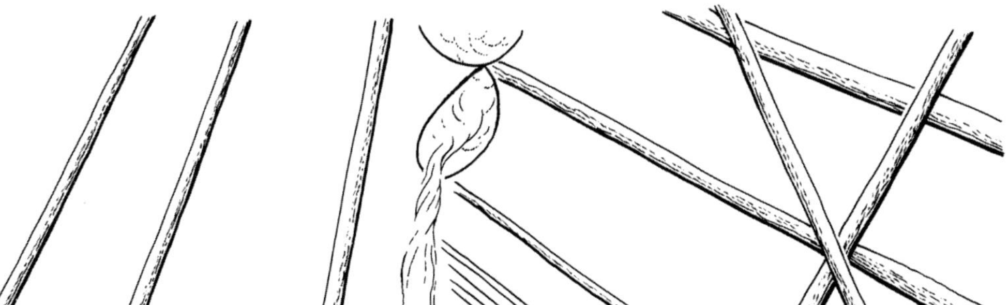

CHAPTER 2

# BLACKFOOT RAIDERS

Before reflecting on the transition effected by firearms, we should widen our study to include another important Northern tribe, the Blackfoot. Blackfoot land was traditionally further west and south than that of the Cree, with a north–south range of the Saskatchewan River in Alberta, down to the plains of Montana, and reaching as far west as the Rocky Mountains.

Around 1800, the Blackfoot were estimated to number a minimum of 20,000 people (according to a report to the US Secretary of War), and they were much feared by both American settlers and associated tribes. American trappers encroaching into Blackfoot territory during the early 1800s did so at risk of their lives, and Blackfoot war parties were known for their extreme prejudice in going after their goals. Some war parties were known to travel hundreds of kilometres for an engagement. Yet the historian John C. Ewers has emphasized that like many Native American tribes, even the Blackfoot waged war with only limited aims:

**MOUNTED BLACKFOOT WARRIOR**
A Blackfoot warrior shows his skills with a horse while carrying a musket. Although the Native Americans readily adopted both firearms and horses, the two were an awkward mix, especially if the warrior attempted to reload the flintlock gun on horseback. For this reason, Native Americans often stuck with their traditional bows when fighting from horses, until the percussion age.

**Blackfoot Horse Raiding Outfit**
This group of Blackfoot raiders travel light, equipped with little more than bedrolls, a pouch for ammunition and supplies, and sheath knives. During long-distance raids, such parties would traditionally live off the land, something the settlers were generally unable to do.

"Nevertheless, Blackfoot warfare was aimed at neither the systematic extermination of enemy tribes nor the acquisition of their territory. It was not organized and directed by a central military authority, nor was it prosecuted by large, disciplined armies. Rather, Blackfoot warfare was carried on primarily by small parties of volunteers who banded together to capture horses from enemy tribes. Each raiding party was hastily organized before departure and disbanded immediately after its return home. It might never see action again as a military unit. Its members were motivated much less by tribal patriotism than by hope of personal gain—the economic security and social prestige that possession of a goodly number of horses would bring them. The killing of enemy tribesmen and the taking of scalps were not major objectives of these raids."

– *John C. Ewers* (1958)

**Preparation**

Blackfoot warfare, therefore, was predatory but not overly destructive in its goals. To back up his point, Ewers described in detail the process of a horse-raiding party, a useful study for the general theme of horse raiding that occurs throughout this book. Raiding tended to be more common in the spring and summer months, as better weather made travelling easier, although Ewers points out that winter raids might be conducted because of the reduced vigilance of 'enemy' tribes and the sound-masking effects of deep snowfall. The party would be organized and led by an experienced warrior, who gathered volunteers for the raid. Participation was not compulsory, but there was doubtless some social pressure on a young man to join in unless he had good reason not to.

Typically the Blackfoot party would amount to around a dozen men. The raiders would not set out immediately, but

◀ **In this 1898 photograph, Assiniboine Chief Wets It is shown wearing the traditional feathered and horned headdress, plus a decorated shield. Shield construction varied, but often consisted of a thick disk of wood and/or animal hide.**

**INDIAN WAR PARTY**
The Native American warriors of the far north were adept at coping with snowy conditions. The party here, moving out on a raiding operation, are all wearing snowshoes. Cree Native American snowshoes could measure up to nearly 6 feet (1.8m) long, while those of tribes further north were typically shorter, and triangular or circular in shape. Spears were particularly common weapons of the Northern tribes, as they were used in the hunting of both aquatic and large land animals.

would first have to ask and receive permission for the raid from the tribal chief, then participate in the ritualistic aspects of preparation. They would chant war songs to the rhythm of a skin drum, and gather supplies and clothing for the journey, often supplied by eager relatives. While the Eastern tribes, as we have seen, wore some heavy types of rigid body armor, the Blackfoot and most Northern and Plains tribes wore varieties of "soft armor"—thick padded leather or multi-layer buckskin coats. These would later prove of little use against musket balls or bullets but, during their time, provided some measure of protection against arrows and spears.

Yet for many horse raids, especially those during the hot summer months, the raiders were likely to ride "light" without any form of armor, wearing just their traditional buckskin clothing and moccasin footwear. Spare clothes were carried in a separate bag.

In terms of weaponry, the Blackfoot raiding party would also avoid weighing themselves down with an unwarranted armory. The raid, after all, was for acquiring horses rather than engaging in a long battle of attrition. Most warriors would carry a large knife in a sheath at his waist—the metal blades being one of the benefits of trade with the Europeans. This blade was as much a utility tool as a weapon, being used for making camp or cutting rawhide bindings, for example. In addition, the warrior also carried either a bow or a musket. Each weapon had its merits and drawbacks. The bow was lighter and had a higher rate of fire than the musket, but did not carry the shock value, penetration or, with rifled weapons, the range and accuracy of the firearm. Bows also had the added advantage of silence—the noise of a gunshot could carry a long way on the plains and in the forests, and might alert the target tribe to the approaching war party. Some accounts speak of raiding parties leaving any firearms behind with the rest of the tribe, owing to both their value and their increasing usefulness for hunting.

### War Lodges

Ewers notes that: "On approaching enemy territory, the raiders stopped to kill enough game to provide food for the remainder of the journey. Usually they built a war lodge in a heavily timbered bottom or on a thickly wooded height, or repaired an old one built by some earlier party." War lodges were not necessarily defensive fortifications *per se*, although they could be turned to that purpose if necessary, but were rather camouflaged and discreet refuges where the raiding

### War Paint

Native Americans applied war paint to the face and body for both spiritual and practical reasons. Spiritually, each tribe had its own symbolism that represented concepts of death (commonly evoked through black paint), bravery, success (often red paint), revenge, and so on. Applying these colors would inspire confidence, courage and resignation to the will of the spirits. The paint also carried talismanic qualities, supposedly helping to ward off enemy blows and missiles. The practical purpose of war paint was that in the heat of battle it helped the tribes to identify their own—something otherwise not easy in tribes with similar styles of dress.

**▲ Ne-Sou-A Quoit, a Fox chief. His face is entirely covered in war paint, the dominant color, red, likely indicating his success as a warrior on the field of battle, or making the intimidating suggestion of future spilt blood. The red coloring was produced by using ochre, a reddish clay, and was painted on using either tree-branch brushes or bone.**

**◀ The Blackfoot chief Mehkskeme-Sukahs, with blood patterns painted onto his face. Red was actually the most popular color of war paint, owing to the wide availability of ochre. Black lines were also favored, created by using a charcoal stick.**

**Blackfoot Medicine Shield**
A medicine shield was not only a tool of physical protection, it also contained spiritual protection for the warrior who carried it. The motifs and decorations on the shield held religious significance for the tribe, and each shield was usually blessed by the village shaman before it was allowed to go into battle.

**Blackfoot Indians with Shields**
Two Blackfoot warriors equipped with wooden medicine shields. Interestingly, the European settlers attempted to sell metal shields to the Blackfoot, but the Blackfoot largely rejected these. They felt that the metal shields were both an extravagance and were spiritually deficient.

party could recuperate and prepare. Nor were they only built by the Blackfoot—war lodges appear to be common among the Plains Indians, and were used by tribes such as the Cree, Sioux, Crow, Cheyenne and Arapaho (see the next chapter for more about the specifics of war on the Plains). The war lodge was a rather rough-and-ready construction. Constructed in a tipi shape, it was usually formed from three or four thick logs or boughs arranged in an upright, mutually supporting structure, with the "walls" made from intertwined branches covered with overlapping sheets of cottonwood bark to provide waterproofing. Alternatively, the warriors might use similar principles to construct a rectangular version. Regardless of the final shape, the war lodge was generally made to blend into the wilderness and its status as a habitation was not apparent at a casual glance. The great American explorers Lewis and Clark, in their work *Travels to the Source of the Missouri River* (1815), recount the appearance of a typical war lodge (not Blackfoot):

"In one of the low bottoms of the river was an Indian fort, which seems to have been built during the last summer. It was built in the form of a circle, about fifty feet [15m] in diameter, five feet high [1.5m], and formed of logs, lapping over each other, and covered on the outside with bark set up on end. The entrance also was guarded by a work on each side of it facing the river. These entrenchments, the squaw informs us, are frequently made by the Minnetarees and other Indians at war with the Shoshonees, when pursued by their enemies on horseback."

—*Lewis and Clark* (1815)

War lodges were essential for raiding parties. It must be remembered that raids were conducted against targets sometimes hundreds of kilometres from the warriors' home village, and the warriors might be living off the land for several weeks.

### The Raid

When approaching the enemy's camp or village, the raiding party detached scouts to go out on reconnaissance, noting details such as enemy strength, weaponry, direction of travel, how many horses were available, and so on. The scouts then reported back to the leader, and a plan of attack was formed. As an attack was usually scheduled for dawn, the attackers would spend a fitful night going through pre-fight rituals, such as singing war songs, applying war paint, praying to the sun and moon for success in combat and putting on war medicine bundles. These bundles were typically pouches containing charms deemed to protect the warrior in battle and life. The objects within the bundles varied from pieces of fur and animal skin through to scalps and pipes. Bunches of feathers tied together might also constitute a medicine bundle (this style of bundle was common among the Blackfoot).

Preparations complete, the warriors would then move in at dawn. The supreme achievement was to stalk silently into the enemy camp, cut the ties of the horses, and lead them equally silently out of the camp. Ewers notes that "forty to sixty horses was considered a very good haul" for their troubles. If the enemy was not awakened during these efforts, the raiders would focus on covering as much ground as quickly as possible to put distance between them and the village—doubtless enemy warriors would set off in pursuit once the theft was discovered, and tracking several dozen fleeing horses was little problem for Native American scouts. If the raiding party was caught in the act, or during the subsequent pursuit, then it would have to fight.

When it came to combat, the raiders had surprise on their side, but usually little else, especially when raiding a well-populated village. Raiding parties were undoubtedly precarious affairs, not only threatening death

◀ **A nineteenth-century portrait of a northern Native American and his son. Note the thick mittens, which were often designed to allow operation of a firearm.**

**NORTHERN SHIELDS**

The following is a description from a French missionary, writing in 1633, describing a Canadian Indian's shield and its use:

"He bore with him a very large buckler, very long and very wide; it covered all my body easily, and went from my feet up to my chest. They raise it and cover themselves entirely with it. It was made of a single piece of very light cedar; I do not know how they can smooth so large and wide a board with their knives; it was a little bent or curved in order the better to cover the body, and in order that the strokes of arrows or of blows coming to split it should not carry away the piece, he had sewed it above and below with cord of skin; they do not carry the shields on the arm; they pass the cord which sustains them over the right shoulder, protecting the left side; and when they have aimed their blow they have only to draw back the right side to cover themselves."

– *Beauchamp* (1905)

▶ **This seventeenth-century woodcut shows a Native American from the Great Lakes area holding a shield and bow, with arrows in a quiver.**

in battle but also the prospect of death from disease or exposure during the long journey. In 1859, the American artist Paul Kane published an account of his travels among the Native American peoples of Canada, and described a Cree and a Blackfoot expedition that ended disastrously for the raiders.

"A year before my arrival amongst them, a war party of 700 left for the Blackfeet country, which nation the Crees regard as their natural enemies, and are never at peace with them. After travelling for some fifteen or twenty days, a sickness broke out among them, affecting numbers and carrying off a few. This was considered by some of their great men a judgment upon them from the Great Spirit for some previous misconduct, and they, therefore, returned home without having accomplished anything. On another occasion a similar party fell in with a great warrior among the Blackfeet, named 'Big Horn', and six of his tribe, who were out on the legitimate calling of horse stealing—for the greater the horse thief the greater the warrior. This small band, seeing their inferiority to their enemies, attempted flight; but finding escape impossible, they instantly dug holes sufficiently deep to intrench themselves, from which they kept up a constant fire with guns and arrows, and for nearly twelve hours held at bay this large war party, bringing down every man who ventured within shot, until their

▲ **Blackfoot warriors clash with Sioux Native Americans on the North American plains. Note the use of spears, shields, tomahawks and handguns, plus the martial decoration on the warriors' horses.**

ammunition and arrows were entirely exhausted, when they of course fell an easy prey to their enemies, thirty of whom had fallen before their fire. This so enraged the Crees that they cut them in pieces, and mangled the dead bodies in a most brutal manner, and carried their scalps back as trophies."

– *Kane* (1859)

Kane's account is an important corrective to some complacent notions about Native American warriors. Although they were often supremely in tune with the landscape, the experience of surviving in the wilderness was still depressingly hard, especially factoring in disease. In one winter alone (1839–40), for example, the Blackfoot lost some 8000 people to smallpox, and most other Native American tribes suffered from similar biological culls. Note also how in the case of the defending Blackfoot, they actually go to ground in what sound like shallow slit trenches. The response to their situation is very modern, and shows that they had no desire to sacrifice themselves needlessly. The Blackfoot capability with firearms is also apparent, and leads us to closer examination of how Native American warfare in general changed with the gun rather than the bow. As we shall see, the Northern Indians bought wholeheartedly into the use of firearms, but blended them with very traditional skills and tactics.

CHAPTER 3

# From Bows to Firearms

In the late eighteenth century, a chief of the Piegan tribe, Saukamappee, described a battle between the Piegan and Shoshone that took place in 1725 near Saskatoon, Saskatchewan. The account is remarkable for providing an insight into pre-contact Native American warfare, particularly the ritualistic aspects of the clash, and also for describing the types of weapons and their use:

"A war chief was elected by the chiefs, and we got ready to march. Our spies had been sent out and had seen a large camp of the Snake [Shoshone] Indians on the Plains of the Eagle Hill, and we had to cross the river in canoes, and on rafts, which we carefully secured for our retreat. When we had crossed and numbered our men, we were about 350 warriors ... they had their scouts out, and came out to meet us. Both parties made a great show of their numbers, and I thought that they were more numerous than ourselves. After some singing and dancing, they sat down on the ground, and placed their large shields before them, which covered them. We did the same, but our shields were not so many, and some of our shields had to shelter two men. Theirs were all placed touching one another; their bows were not so long as ours, but of better wood, and the back covered with the sinews of the bisons which made them very elastic, and their arrows went a long way and whizzed about us as balls do from guns. They were all headed with a sharp, smooth, black stone which broke when it struck anything. Our iron-headed arrows did not go through their shields, but stuck in them. On both sides, several were wounded, but none lay on the ground; and night put an end to the battle, without a scalp being taken on either side, and in those days such was the result, unless one party was more numerous than the other."

In many ways the encounter seems purposely designed to avoid major casualties. The warriors present themselves openly, and then seemingly at some prearranged signal squat down behind shields to exchange arrows. Bows are the primary weapons. The Shoshone Indians shoot flint-headed arrows from sinew-backed bows, while the Piegan seem to be using self-bows. Sinew-backed bows improved the power of the bow by gluing a strip of elastic sinew to the inside of the bow—the sinew increased the whip effect when the bow was released, thereby imparting more power to the arrow. Typically, Northern bows were manufactured from ash or hickory, although some extant Northern bows have been found made from yew or osage orange—both excellent woods that grow well outside of the Northern territories, suggesting that the Northern Native Americans would import high-quality bow woods when possible.

Once firearms spread throughout the Northern territories from the seventeenth century, however, this formalized picture of warfare changed significantly. For a start, the battle of opposing shield lines described above became suicidal for both sides, as the balls of powerful muskets and rifles were capable of punching through the wooden shields and killing the person on the other side. Open confrontation therefore became inadvisable, and instead stealth and speed became the keynotes for successful warmaking. These were tactical effects, but the introduction of firearms also had a strategic effect. For example, as we have seen, the Cree began purchasing firearms from the French and British in the seventeenth century, giving them an advantage in their territory. The nearby Assiniboine tribe, who at that time did not have access to firearms, sensed that a strategic partnership was advisable, and so allied themselves with the Cree. In turn they received firearms, the Cree acting as an intermediary between the Europeans and the Assiniboine. Collectively the partners now embarked on a war against the Dakota (Sioux).

Already faced with the gun-toting Chippewa tribe, the Sioux were driven from the Great Lakes region by the hostile tribes, showing how firearms could alter balances of power that in some cases had existed for centuries. The Cree, Assiniboine and other gun-armed tribes met a more equal match in the form of the Blackfoot, who were also equipped with firearms. The consequence was much more costly engagements for all sides involved, both in terms of casualties and territory lost.

Of course, the acquisition of firearms by the Northern Native Americans also affected the conflict between Indian and settler, which became increasingly virulent as the rapacious settlers absorbed more and more land out west. By the end of the nineteenth century, furthermore, the United States was an established entity and the Federal Government was looking to use all its resources to remove Native American obstructions to the American land-grab. During the 1860s, for example, gold was discovered in Blackfoot territory, leading to a huge influx of prospectors and settlers. By this time, the Blackfoot were tremendously weakened anyway—the continuing destruction of the Plains buffalo by white hunters was not only eroding their wealth, but literally removing their source of sustenance and shelter.

### The Matchlock

As firearms played such an important part in the evolution of Native American warfare, it is useful to explore the evolution of firearms technology between the seventeenth and the nineteenth centuries. During the sixteenth century, when the Native Americans first began to acquire guns, the matchlock arquebus left a great deal to be desired. The matchlock system worked via a smouldering slowmatch (lit prior to the engagement), that was held in a curved piece of metal known as a serpentine. When the trigger was pulled, the serpentine fell forwards under spring power and dropped the match into an exposed pan of priming powder. The match detonated the priming powder, the consequent flame passed down a vent hole into the main chamber, where it ignited the principal powder charge to fire the gun. The loading process was slow, infuriatingly so in battle conditions as the shooter had to ram powder, wad and ball down the barrel, prime the pan with powder, blow on the match, and cock the serpentine, after which he could then actually aim and fire.

But this was not the end of the problems associated with the matchlock. They were shockingly inaccurate, with an effective range of about 25m (82ft). The need to keep powder and match dry for the gun to be effective presented serious difficulties during winter, or in the damp woodland conditions of the east and the north. The Native Americans understood this flaw, as the English explorer Henry Hudson discovered in 1607:

"The Salvadges [savages] perceiving so much, subtiley devised how they might put out the fire [the burning match] ... by which means they sawe they should be free from the danger of our mens pieces [guns] ... one of the salvadges came ... and taking the fier-brand which one of our company held in his hand ... he presently therew it into the water."

Although there is some evidence of Native Americans using early firearms against settlers as early as the time of Hudson's experience, the matchlock arquebus probably impressed them more on account of its bang and smoke than its combat performance. Yet in time things would change. Beginning in the sixteenth century, the quality of gunpowder improved through the process of "corning"—mixing the constituents with water and letting the mix dry into a large "cake," which was then crumbled up into regularly sized granules. By achieving a more uniform mix of the ingredients, and providing air gaps between each granule of powder, "corned" gunpowder burned faster and hence produced far greater levels of power, increasing the penetration provided and presented a more effective threat to Native American shields and armor.

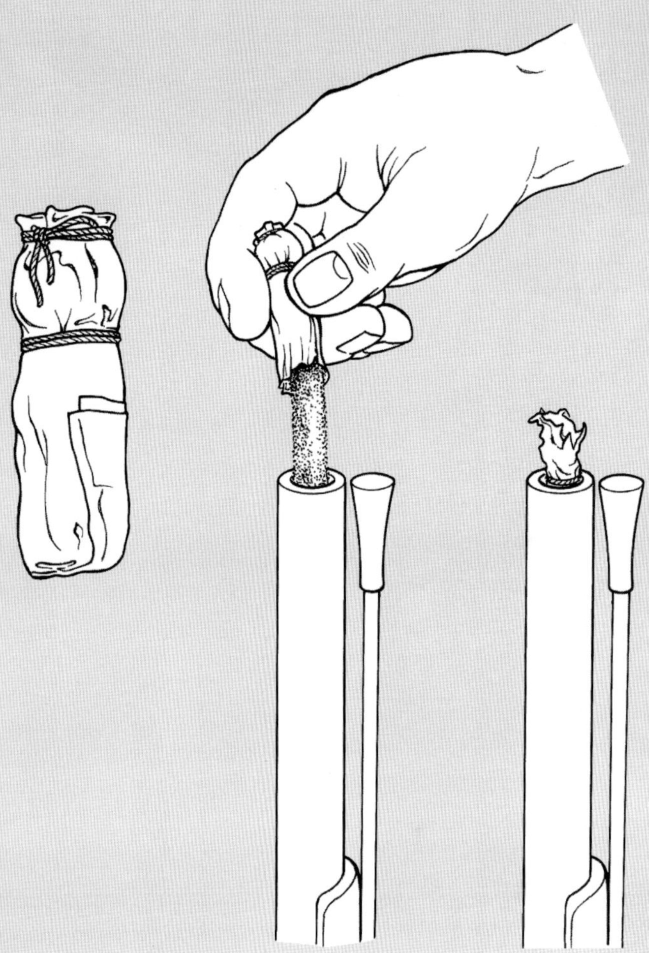

**Loading Procedures**
The muzzle-loading procedure began with tearing open a paper cartridge and pouring the power into the barrel, saving a small amount to prime the pan. The wad and ball were then rammed down onto the powder, the hammer cocked and the gun was ready to fire.

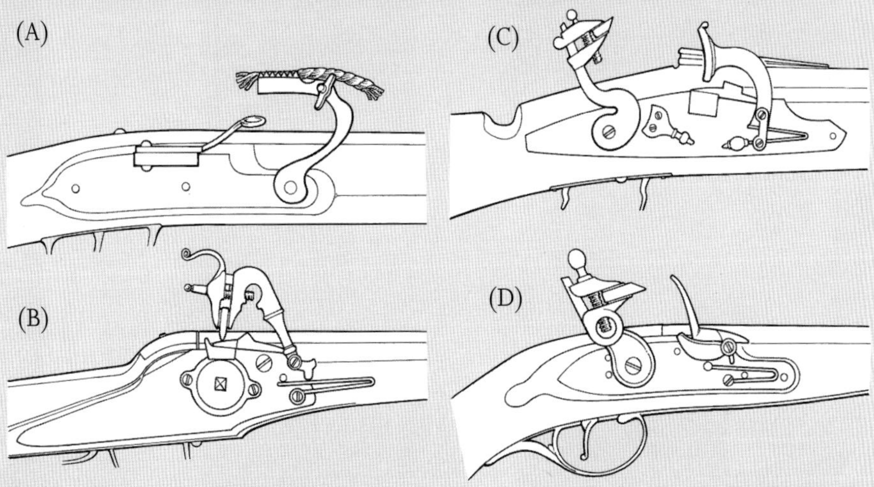


**Firing Mechanisms**
The four major firearms ignition systems of the pre-percussion age were: (A) Matchlock; (B) Wheellock; (C) Snaphance; (D) Flintlock. Native Americans were seen with all the types apart from wheellocks, which were expensive items to purchase even for Europeans, and were fragile when used in field conditions.

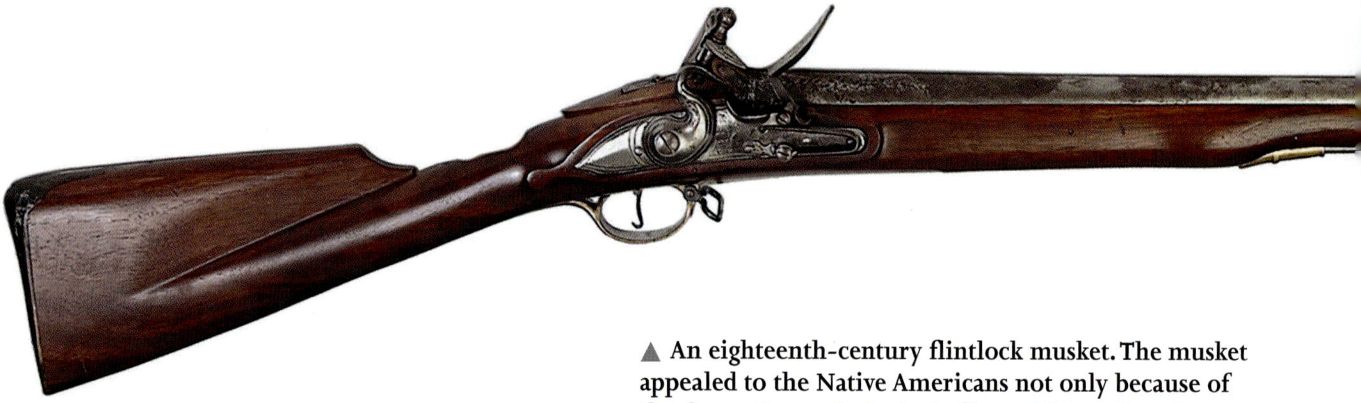

▲ An eighteenth-century flintlock musket. The musket appealed to the Native Americans not only because of the dramatic psychological effect of firing, but also because of its range and penetration, useful for both hunting and warfare.

### The Flintlock

A more important innovation for the Native Americans, however, was the introduction of the flintlock, which entered firearms history around 1630. The flintlock did away with the need for a smouldering slowmatch. In its place came a spring locked "cock" that gripped a piece of flint. The gun was muzzle-loaded in much the same way as previous weapons, but when the trigger was pulled the cock dropped forward under spring pressure and the flint struck a steel set over the priming pan. The sparks created by the flint hitting the steel ignited the primer and fired the gun.

For the Native Americans, as for the Europeans, the flintlock had several far-reaching advantages over its predecessor. First, combined with the improvements in gunpowder, the flintlock was a more reliable weapon that was not susceptible to the vagaries of a smouldering match. The flint would, to a large extent, work regardless of the weather, although there was still the need to keep powder dry. Furthermore,

▲ A group of Alaskan Native Americans, here seen photographed at the end of the nineteenth century, stand in front of totem poles. The warriors are armed with a mix of flintlock and percussion weapons.

ignition was faster, and the knock-on effect was to make firearms more accurate, as there was less time for the shooter to wobble off target when he pulled the trigger. Flintlocks were also more practical propositions for both hunting and warfare because there was no glowing match to alert the prey or enemy. This was particularly important to the Native Americans, who conducted most of their hunting and warfare around daybreak, when light levels were still low and any bright object showed up clearly.

Finally, combined with the eventual standardization of firearms that accompanied the growth of mass armies, flintlocks became cheaper and more accessible to the Native Americans. In fact, on many occasions the colonizers issued edicts prohibiting the trading of weapons with the Native Americans. A British edict of 1641, for example, stated that: "In trucking or trading with the Indians no man shall give them for any commodity of their, silver or gold, or any weapons of war, either guns or gunpowder, nor sword ... which might come to be used against ourselves." Such restrictions had only a limited effect on the number of firearms in Native American hands. Rather, in many respects, the Native Americans eventually became known as useful gunsmiths, repairing lock mechanisms or using their superb woodworking skills to manufacture or mend stocks.

Because the Native American style of warfare preferred accuracy over volley firing, the Native Americans came to value high-quality weapons, although they purchased more than their fair share of "trade guns." These were cheap guns manufactured mostly for the Native American market, styled on French military muskets, albeit with reduced dimensions to cut the costs of production and transport. The firearms historian Carl Parcher Russell here describes the typical features of this type of gun:

"The trade gun came from many different factories in Europe and the United States. Regardless of its point of origin, certain characteristics were constant. First of all, it was often light in weight, often short of barrel, and cheaply constructed. Commonly it was gauged to shoot a one-ounce ball; that is, it was sixteen-gauge, or about .66 caliber, although some were smaller. The trigger guard was clumsy in appearance and was large enough to permit access to the trigger even though the finger was enclosed in a glove or mitten. It was a gun made for the north country."

– *Parcher Russell* (1980)

Although trade guns were a little rough and ready, they were tailored to Native American requirements, particularly those, as Parcher Russell points out, of the Northern territories. By being light and short they were more easily carried through the wilderness and more easily used from horseback, in the same manner as a cavalry carbine. The ability to shoot the gun while wearing a thick glove or mitten would also appeal to those Native Americans of the far north, who had to hunt or fight in the winter.

### Rifles

Yet as we have seen, the Indian warrior also valued accuracy, and trade guns were not accurate—typical

▲ A Native American buying weapons from settlers at the end of the eighteenth century; here he cautiously tests the flintlock mechanism. Settlers were more than willing to trade cheap guns for expensive furs.

**RIEL'S REBELLIONS** 1816–85

**The Métis rebellions led by Louis Riel produced a string of battles along the Canadian border. Although the Métis won major battles at places such as Fish Creek, a series of defeats in 1885 brought the rebellion to an end.**

effective range would have been 164–328 ft (50–100m), depending on the quality of the barrel, sights and ball. Far more appealing to the Native Americans was a decent quality rifle. Rifling consisted of spiral grooves cut into the bore of a weapon, these imparting gyroscopic spin to a projectile, dramatically improving its flight characteristics and therefore its accuracy and effective range. The European ancestry of rifling is much debated, but what is certain is that during the seventeenth century German gunmakers had perfected a short-barrelled flintlock rifle known to history as the Jäger rifle. This was a true hunter's weapon (their expense prohibiting widespread military use), relatively easy to carry in the field and capable of genuine accuracy out to 200m (656ft). German immigrants into Pennsylvania and Kentucky began producing their own local versions of the Jäger rifle, resulting in the famous "Kentucky" or "Pennsylvania" rifle of American lore.

CHAPTER 4

# Riel's Rebellions

The skills of both European and Native American warfare were combined in the Métis, persons of mixed French-Canadian and Native American ancestry who principally settled during the eighteenth century in Saskatchewan and Manitoba. The Métis lifestyle was a blend of cultures, mixing European-style agriculture with regular hunting and trapping expeditions, the latter involving the use of tipis for temporary housing.

Métis people relied heavily upon the fur trade for income, and hence came into conflict with the Hudson's Bay Company during the 1840s. The Company had a monopoly on fur trading in the area, and wanted to stop the Métis taking their goods to market in the United States. The outcome was a series of rebellions at first led by Louis Riel, a French-Ojibway businessman. The so-called "Courthouse Rebellion" of 1849, a violent march on a courthouse in Fort Garry, began the protests, which were continued by Riel's son, Louis David Riel, from the late 1860s, when an influx of settlers threatened long-standing Métis land ownership. In 1869, Riel Jr and his "border patrol" captured Fort Garry and by 1870 Riel had forced the Canadian government's hand, and was governor of his province. Yet Riel's political fortunes turned, and he was exiled in 1870, only returning in 1876.

The situation for the Métis worsened during the 1880s, when the Canadian-Pacific Railway began to cut through Métis territory and bring more settlers onto their land. In 1885, another Métis rebellion began, this time aided by an uprising of equally aggrieved Cree Native Americans. The scale of violence was far greater than previously. Cree warriors massacred nine settlers near Frog Lake, Saskatchewan, on April 2 and also defeated a Gatling-gun armed force of regulars at Cut Knife on May 2. The Métis achieved their own victories, such as that at Fish Creek on April 24, but the scale of Canadian forces soon proved overwhelming, with a serious defeat at Batoche on May 9. With the Cree collapse at Loon Lake in June 1885, both the Cree and the Métis rebellion withered, and Riel was captured and hanged.

For the Native Americans who could obtain them, the Kentucky rifle was a superb hunting weapon that was incidentally perfectly suited to their sniping and ambushing style of warfare. Detailed accounts of the Northern Native American use of rifles are few and far between, but we catch some glimpses of their effectiveness. Published in 1839, Hugh Murray's *An historical and descriptive account of British America* describes the battles for Quebec that occurred during the Seven Years' War. In the following passage, he explains one of the failed attempts by the British to take Quebec in 1759:

"In 1759 preparations were made on a great scale for the conquest of Canada, comprising twenty sail of the line, with smaller vessels and transports, having on board 8000 veteran troops. These were placed under the direction of Wolfe, who was allowed the choice of all his officers. After a prosperous voyage the armament, on June 26, arrived off the Isle of Orleans. Quebec was defended by the Marquis de Montcalm, having under his command 13,000 men, of whom indeed only 2000 were regular troops, the rest being Canadian militia, with a few Indians. The attack having been long foreseen, full time was given him to entrench and strengthen his position ... Montcalm, strongly posted between Quebec and Montmorenci, poured in upon them a destructive fire; the Indian rifle told with fatal effect; and the assailants were finally repulsed with the loss of 182 killed and 650 wounded."

– *Murray* (1839)

Although the account was written some years after the event, it is interesting that Murray highlights the role of the "Indian rifle," in spite of the fact that the

▲ A dramatic reconstruction of the Riel Rebellions shows Canadian troops attacking Métis forces. Although the Métis had plenty of firearms, they faced troops armed with field artillery.

Native American element of Montcalm's force was small compared to his regular troops. Other accounts around this time bear out the respect that the settlers had for Northern Native American marksmanship. An article in *Wadie's Select Circulating Library*, published in Pennsylvania in 1833, describes the construction of a French fort at Detroit, the layout of the building obviously respecting the marksman who might watch from the surrounding woods:

"The fort of Detroit, as it was originally constructed by the French, stands in the middle of a common, or description of small prairie, bordered by woods, which were at that time untouched by the hand of civilisation. Erected at a distance of about half a mile [0.8km] from the banks of the river, which at that particular point are high and precipitous, it stood then just far enough from the woods that swept round it in a semicircular form to be secure from the rifle of the Indian."

There is little doubt, therefore, that the settlers both feared and respected Northern Native Americans' capabilities with firearms. In the next chapter, we will continue our study of the Native American relationship with guns by looking at the percussion weapons of the nineteenth century, and how they affected the fight for the frontier. But at this point we need to venture further north and west, and see how the new ways of warfare affected the most isolated of the Native American tribes.

**Fort St. Charles**
Fort St. Charles, established by the French on the Canadian–US border in the eighteenth century, exemplifies the challenge the Native Americans faced when attacking settler fortifications. Cannon cover nearly every line of approach to the fort, and elevated firing platforms provided good fields of fire to infantry.

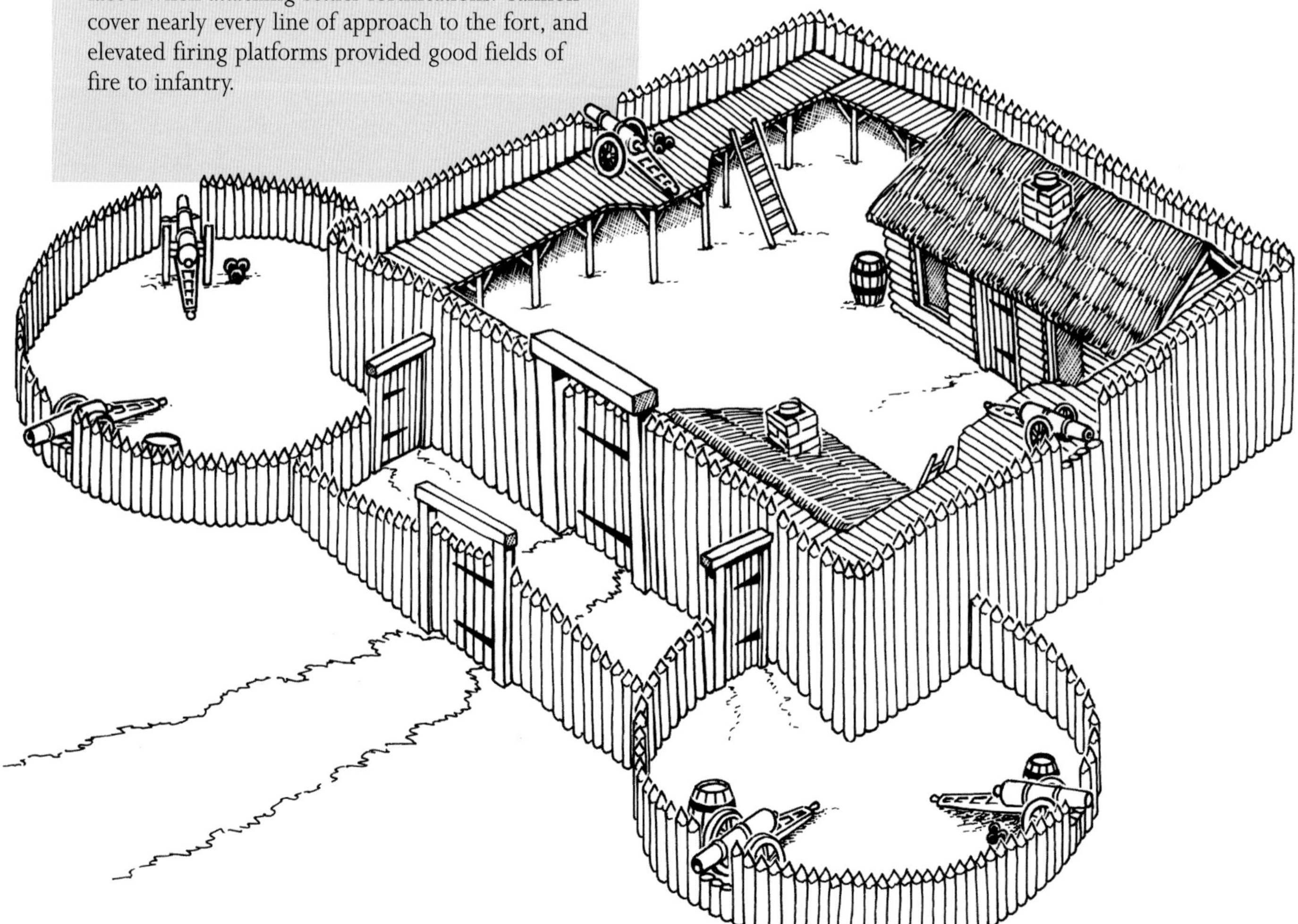

CHAPTER 5

# Arctic and Subarctic Warriors

The far reaches of North America contain some of the most inhospitable wildernesses in the world. In the subarctic and Arctic Circle, reaching from Alaska in the west to north-eastern Canada, the combination of sub-zero temperatures, bitterly cruel and long winters, frequently scarce food supplies and thin vegetation meant that only the hardiest of Native American tribes survived there. Yet survive they did. Tribes that inhabited these unforgiving lands included the Inuit, Kutchin, Hare and Yellowknife, plus several others. Nor did the austerity of their environment prevent the settlers from eventually moving up into their space. Contact between Alaskans and Siberians/Russians went back for millennia, but the European settlers also ventured far north.

**▲ Indigenous Alaskan people outside the Hudson's Bay Company trading post at Fort Yukon. As well as desirable goods, the settlers also brought disease and alcohol to the Northern Native American tribes, slashing their numbers and weakening any armed resistance.**

**Inuit Warrior and Equipment**
This Inuit warrior is well equipped for Arctic hunting or warfare. The impressively sized snowshoes would give mobility over the deepest snow, while the rifle is wrapped in a fur-lined gun case (top right). The guncase was essential for stopping the gun mechanism getting wet then freezing solid.

▲ **Sinew-backed Inuit bows carried formidable powers of range and penetration, the latter demonstrated by this large polar bear kill.**

The Hudson's Bay Company was working up into the Arctic Circle by the eighteenth century, and the Klondike Gold Rush of the late nineteenth century drew more than 40,000 Americans up into Alaska and Canada. Yet the far Northern tribes of North America are a distinctive part of our study. Although they came into contact with the settlers, sometimes violently so, and adopted modern tools such as firearms, the isolation of many of the tribes meant that many of the older fighting methods were preserved for much longer than elsewhere.

## Warrior Ethos

As well as fighting the climate, the far Northern Indians also spent a proportion of their time in minor warfare with each another, usually in brief but murderous clashes over issues such as fishing grounds or feuds. Because food was in such tight supply, the battles could be prosecuted with extreme focus, and casualties could be high. The warrior ethos was consequently high in such communities. Here Waldemar Bogoras, an ethnographer who studied the Chuchkee tribe of Siberia, describes the inculcation of warrior values and skills in the young warrior. The study is relevant to this book because of the close cultural similarities and historical relationship between the Siberian aborigines and the Alaskan Native Americans:

"To be fit for fighting, every warrior undergoes hard training, and spends all his leisure in various exercises ... The hero must run for long distances, drawing a heavily-loaded sledge. He carries stone and timber, jumps up in the air, but above all, he fences with his long spear. He performs this exercise quite alone; and the chief feature of it is the brandishing of the spear with the utmost force, so that it bends like a piece of raw reindeer leg-skin. He also practices shooting with the bow, and uses for this purpose in various arrows, sharp and blunt. From all these exercises he acquires great skill and agility ... When he is shot at, he avoids the arrows by springing to one side, or parries them all with the butt-end of the spear, or simply catches them between his fingers and throws them back."

– *Bogoras* (1909)

The account of this martial training evokes images of the Spartans of ancient Greece creating the perfect warrior, a potent mixture of raw physical power and skill at arms.

## Weapons and Armour

Two particular weapons are mentioned in Bogoras's account—the bow and the spear. Of the former, the wood available to the tribes of the far north was frequently unsuited to making self-bows, weakened as they were by constant damp or extremely cold temperatures. Many bows, therefore, were of the composite type, made from spruce driftwood enhanced by the addition of strips of bone, sinew or rawhide to improve their strength and elastic properties, and hence their power.

**▼ Inuits with spears hunt for fish in a river. The same spears could be applied in warfare, and were often thrown using atlatl launchers.**

▲ An Inuit storage box plus two traditional weapons—an axe consisting of a sharpened stone bound to a shaft, and a "knife" created from a piece of carved bone. Both would be lethal when wielded with purpose.

Adventurer John Murdoch, writing for *Popular Science* magazine in 1897, explained in detail the structure of the "Eskimoo" bow during his trip into Alaska in 1891.

"As everyone knows, the Eskimoos, with very few exceptions, inhabit a region which is perfectly treeless, or at any rate where nothing grows but pines and spruces, whose soft, inelastic wood is entirely useless for making bows. They have overcome this difficulty very effectively by fastening along the back of the bow twisted cords of reindeer sinew in such a way that each cord is stretched when the bow is bent and flies back when the bow-string is released. As far as we know, no other race of savages makes use of this ingenious contrivance. Some tribes of Indians are in the habit of stiffening their bows by 'backing' them with strips of sinew, glued on, but the Eskimoo backing is made of cords and tied on."

– Murdoch (1897)

Murdoch went on to observe that the power of these bows was actually formidable. Using arrows tipped with bone, flint or metal, the bow was, according to Murdoch, capable of being 'driven

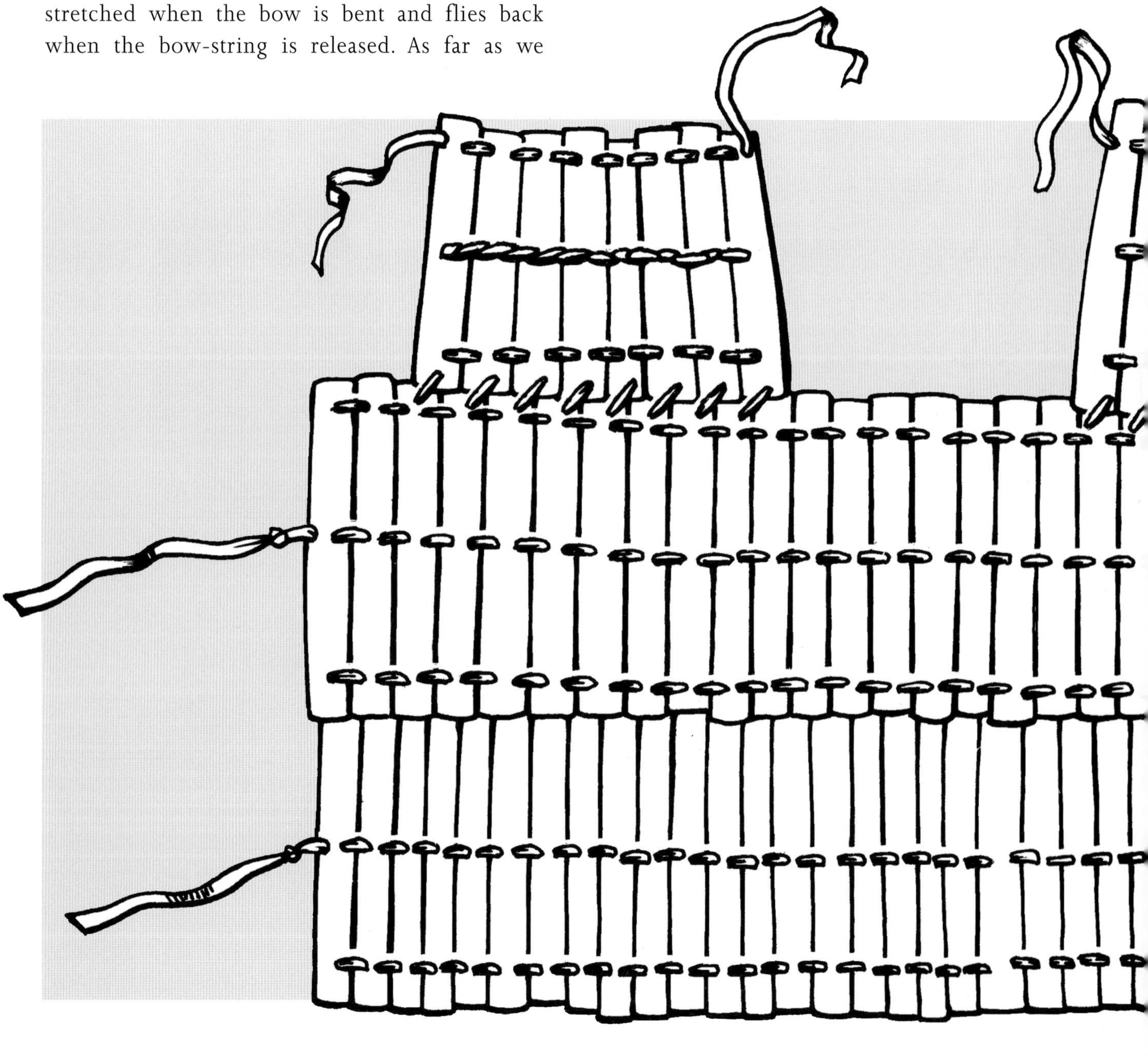

through the body of a polar bear' if there was no bone to obstruct its passage.

Murdoch's article is doubly interesting because it also reflects on the status of the bow in terms of its relation to the rifle, which by the late nineteenth century was part of Inuit life and warfare. He stated that every Inuit hunter "had a pretty good rifle" despite "a law against selling breech-loading arms and ammunition to "Indians," a law he says "was no better enforced in Alaska than it was in old times on the plains." Yet the poverty of the community meant that rifles were still beyond the means of many, hence bows remained important tools even beyond the period covered by this book.

Spears held an equal significance for the tribes of the far north, as they were integral to hunting large coastal or tundra animals such as caribou, seals, whales, deer and moose (plus humans, of course). While the atlatl spear-thrower may have had limited use in the woods of eastern North America, in the subarctic and Arctic zones it was an essential tool of hunting or warfare.

Observers of the Aleut tribe, which was concentrated in the far west of Alaska and in Siberia, noted in 1761 that the warriors could throw spears measuring up to 1.4m (4ft 6in)

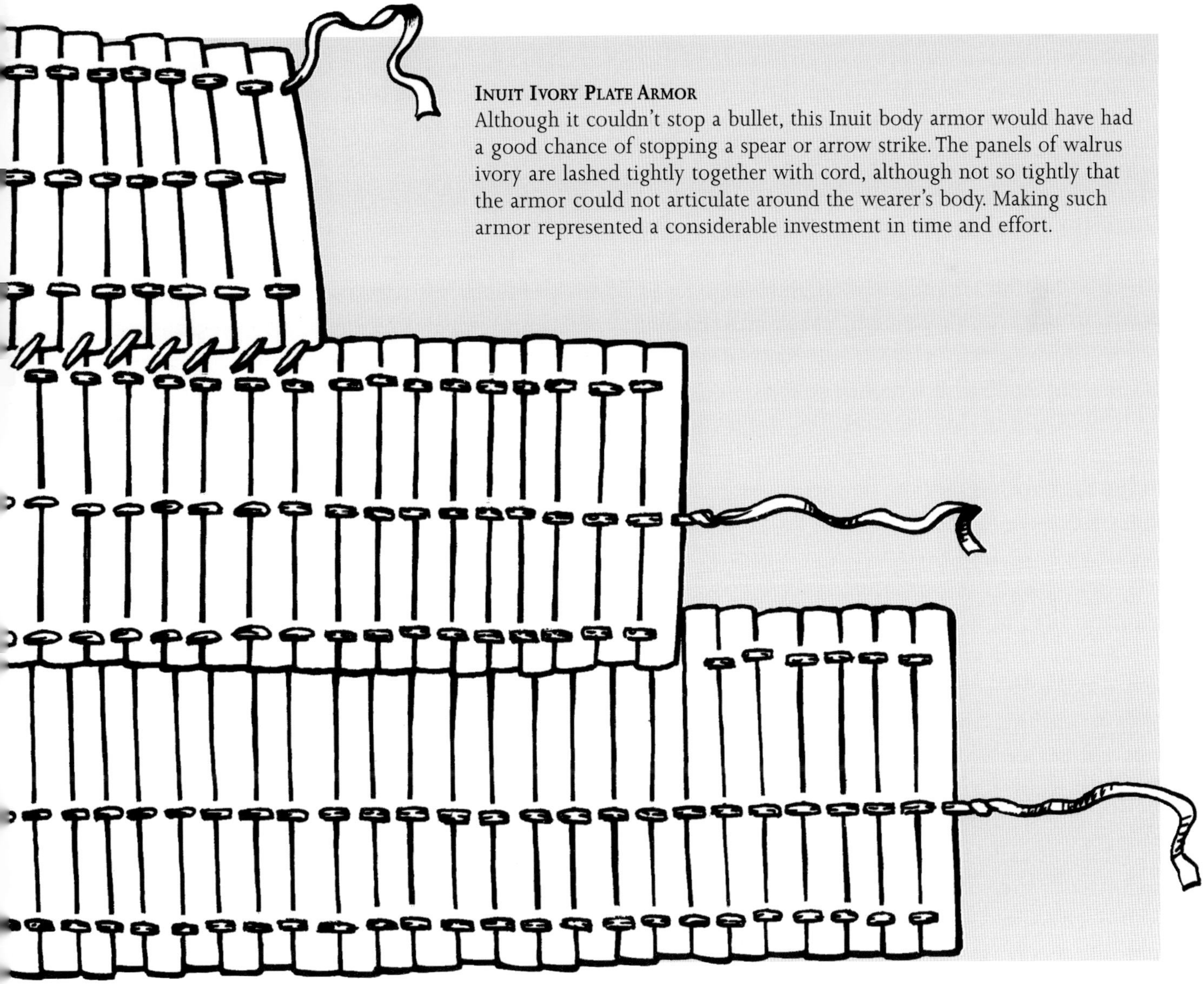

**Inuit Ivory Plate Armor**
Although it couldn't stop a bullet, this Inuit body armor would have had a good chance of stopping a spear or arrow strike. The panels of walrus ivory are lashed tightly together with cord, although not so tightly that the armor could not articulate around the wearer's body. Making such armor represented a considerable investment in time and effort.

accurately to distances of 73–82m (80–90yd). Bearing in mind that in this period of history such range and accuracy outclassed many contemporary firearms, it is little wonder that the far Northern tribes retained their spears all the way into the twentieth century. Note also that the spear tips, made from iron or bone, were sometimes poisoned to improve their killing effect.

Apart from spears and bows, the Northern Indians fought each other with a wide range of other tools. Various types of club feature prominently, which were as much use for despatching injured animals as they were for combat. The clubs were either solid wooden weapons featuring ball-swellings at one end, or adze-type weapons featuring a sharp stone, metal or antler "blade." In addition to these, warriors also used bola missiles. These were made from lengths of rawhide with stones tied to each end, which were then thrown in a spinning motion. Originally bolas were devised to bring down running animals, principally by wrapping the rawhide lengths around the legs, but they could do likewise to running people, the stones causing severe impact injuries while the rawhide could lacerate the body as it wrapped round.

In response to this grim array of projectile and stabbing weapons, it was common for the tribes of the far north to wear some sort of body armor. This came in some unique forms. In the Northern Pacific area, we find examples of warriors wearing knee-length suits of armor made from concentric rings of thick hide sewn together. The design had a telescopic effect, so the warrior could reach down and gather up the lower rings if he wanted to leave his legs free for running. Over this armor was a wide "cape" made from wood and sealskin, which literally formed a U-shaped shield around the warrior's shoulders, upper back and head.

More typically, the body armor of the subarctic and Arctic tribes consisted of bone, wood or walrus-ivory slats sewn together in flexible plates and hung over the shoulders, chest and back. In some cases, matching arm-guards or greaves provided protection to the limbs. Material ingenuity characterized Northern armor. In some cases, armor was made by coating a thick animal skin with glue, to which stones and sand were stuck, creating an extremely tough material. Obviously such armor only had limited effectiveness against the increasingly effective firearms of the period, but against clubs, arrows and spears the protection afforded probably could make the difference between life and death.

### Combat in the Frozen North

Although the scale of warfare in the far North did not reach that experienced by the Eastern and Plains Indians, on a local level it was brutally enacted. David Jones has described a typical raiding action by the Alaskan Kutchin warriors. As with Indian tribes elsewhere, the Kutchin would often fight in small raiding parties, typically in springtime when it was easier to travel, but remaining ice still made it possible to walk across rivers. The procedure for organizing the attack was particularly ritualistic:

"Led by a band headman or a man known for his prowess as a war leader, the raid would be instigated by someone with the grievance. He or she notified the potential war leader, who, in turn, selected three subleaders. The family instigating the fight presented the leader with a wolverine pelt, which he cut into strips and gave to each man, who wrapped one around his head. This act signifies his willingness to partake in the action, as well as connecting him to the wolverine, one of the most ferocious animals of the subarctic forests."

– *Jones* (2004)

Once assembled and embarked upon its raid, a war party, typically no more than 20 or 30 men strong, would descend upon the enemy village or camp at first light. In coordinated fashion, the raiders surged forward and attacked the enemy, using knives and spears to penetrate the skin of the tents, clubbing any who emerged or shooting down those who fled using bows or rifles. Mutilations of the bodies were common (it had ritualistic connotations of weakening the physical strength of the enemy), and Jones notes that all individuals in the camp—men, women and children—would be attacked.

Such a raid inspired a desire for revenge in the victims, and so led to decades of feuding between tribes that cost many lives. Edward Curtis' 1930 study of the Nunivak people of the Bering Strait paints a picture of equal brutality. A classic tactic was to surround the enemy cabins or tents, then bowmen would shoot into the habitations through the smoke holes. Those who were not immediately killed by these volleys had a naturally strong inclination to flee outside, where they were met by waiting Nunivak armed with clubs, spears and other weapons. All males were to be killed, while the women and children were taken as slaves or adopted into Nunivak families deprived of manpower by war. In return, the Nunivak were raided themselves. In one particularly ghastly account, enemy Indians attacked a Nunivak village while the men were out hunting: "They entered all the houses and killed the women and children. Some of the bodies they wrapped in sealskins and threw them into the fires [attacking Indians often torched the habitations]. Most of the children were hurled into the stagnant tundra water. The enemy tied throngs to the arms and legs of one old man and pulled him limb from limb" (Curtis, 1930). In retaliation, Nunivak warriors attacked the enemy camp, and killed everyone there.

The behaviour of the far Northern tribes does illustrate that Native Americans were capable, on occasions, of wars of annihilation against enemy tribes. Against the material depredations of the European settlers, however, they had little defence. European exploitation of whaling grounds, caribou herds and other natural resources, plus the introduction of fatal diseases, took a hideous toll on the Native Americans populations of the far north, and they consequently caused far fewer problems to settler expansion than the tribes of the Great Plains.

# Glossary

**austerity** Lacking luxury and consisting solely of restrained resources.

**carbine** A rifle of short length that historically was used by cavalry.

**consolidating** Strengthening or making many parts into a cohesive unit.

**depredations** Attacks.

**despatching** Killing.

**exposure** Left out in the open or a cause of death that means hypothermia.

**flint** A rock that when hit against steel can cause a spark.

**greave** Armor that fits around the shin.

**hickory** A type of tree that bears nuts and contains seventeen to nineteen species.

**matchlock arquebus** A long gun that required its match to be lit in order to fire.

**muzzle** The end of a gun where the bullet flies out.

**palisades** Long, pointed stakes that are placed next to each other to form a defensive barrier.

**precarious** Likely to be vanquished; living an uncertain or insecure existence.

**prospector** A person who goes to a land seeking to find gold.

**reconnaissance** Attempting to quietly gain information on an enemy or target's position.

**scalping** Cutting off a person's scalp.

**scout** To discreetly survey a place in order to collect information about it that the surveyor will share with his group; a person who does this surveying.

**sinew** A tendon.

**trench** A dug-out line of land that offered refuge from enemy fire.

# FURTHER READING

Belmessous, Saliha. *Empire by Treaty: Negotiating European Expansion, 1600-1900.* Oxford, UK, and New York, NY: Oxford University Press, 2015.

Carew-Miller, Anna. *Native American Cooking.* Philadelphia, PA: Mason Crest, 2014.

Chesterfield, Jayson. *Inuit* (Spotlight on Native Americans). New York, NY: Rosen Publishing, 2016.

Cohen, Robert. *Canada's First Nations and Cultural Genocide* (Bearing Witness: Genocide and Ethnic Cleansing in the Modern World). New York, NY: Rosen Publishing, 2017.

Conrad, Margaret, Alvin Finkel, and Donald Fyson. *History of the Canadian Peoples: Volume 1: Beginnings to 1867.* Toronto, ON: Pearson, 2015.

Dubinsky, Karen, Adele Perry, and Henry Yu. *Within and Without the Nation: Canadian History as Transnational History.* Toronto, ON: University of Toronto Press, 2015.

Dunbar-Ortiz, Roxanne, and Dina Gilio-Whitaker. *"All the Real Indians Died Off" and 20 Other Myths About Native Americans.* Boston, MA: Beacon Press, 2016.

Ferrara, Nadia. *Reconciling and Rehumanizing Indigenous-Settler Relations: An Applied Anthropological Perspective.* Lanham, MD: Lexington Books, 2015.

Gibson, Dale, and Osgoode Society for Canadian Legal History. *Law, Life, and Government at Red River.* Montreal, QC: McGill-Queen's University Press and Toronto, ON: The Osgoode Society for Canadian Legal History, 2015.

Grenfell Price, A. *White Settlers and Native Peoples: An Historical Study of Racial Contacts Between English-speaking Whites and Aboriginal Peoples in the United States, Canada, Australia and New Zealand.* Cambridge, UK: Cambridge University Press, 2015.

Keating, Susan Katz. *Native American Rivalries.* Philadelphia, PA: Mason Crest, 2014.

Klein, Barry T. *Reference Encyclopedia of the American Indian*. Boca Raton, FL: Todd Publications, 2014.

Owsley, Douglas W., and Richard L. Jantz. *Kennewick Man: The Scientific Investigation of an Ancient American Skeleton.* College Station, TX: Texas A & M University Press, 2014.

Razack, Sherene. *Dying from Improvement: Inquests and Inquiries into Indigenous Deaths in Custody.* Toronto, ON: University of Toronto Press, 2015.

Ross, Jeffrey Ian. *American Indians at Risk*. Santa Barbara, CA: Greenwood, 2014.

United States Office of Indian Affairs. *A Guide to Tracing American Indian & Alaska*

*Native Ancestry.* Washington, DC: Office of Public Affairs-Indian Affairs, 2014.
Wakim Dennis, Yvonne, Arlene B. Hirschfelder, and Shannon Rothenberger Flynn. *Native American Almanac: More Than 50,000 Years of the Cultures and Histories of Indigenous Peoples.* Canton, MI: Visible Ink Press, 2016.

**Websites**

Canadian Indian Tribes and Languages: First Nations by Province
http://www.native-languages.org/canada.htm
This website's interactive map offers information about recognized and unrecognized tribes in continental Canada.

EagleFeatherNews
http://www.eaglefeathernews.com
This news site discusses current affairs in Saskatchewan's First Nation and Métis communities.

NativeWeb Resources: Law & Legal Issues
https://www.nativeweb.org/resources/law_legal_issues/index.html
This NativeWeb page offers links to primary sources on the history of various indigenous tribes.

# INDEX


**A**

Alaska, 6, 8, 9, 35, 37–38, 40–43
Aleut, 41
Algonquin, 8, 9, 10
American Revolution, 13
Arapahoe, 21
Arctic Circle, 35, 37
armor, 19, 27, 41, 42
Assiniboine, 8, 26

**B**

Beaver Wars, 10–11, 13
Bering Strait, 9, 43
Blackfoot, 6, 8, 26
    warfare methods, 16–24
bola missiles, 42
bows, 16, 19, 24, 25, 38, 40, 41, 42, 43
British, 8, 11, 13, 29

**C**

canoes, 14, 25
Champlain, Samuel de, 9, 10
Cheyenne, 21
Chippewa, 8, 11, 26
Cree, 6, 8, 13–14, 16, 19, 21, 23, 26, 32
Crow, 21
Curtis, Edward, 43
Cut Knife, 32

**F**

First Nations, how they are classified, 8
Fish Creek, 31, 32
flintlock musket, features of, 28–29
French, 8, 10, 11, 13, 32
French and Indian War, 11
fur, 9, 10, 11, 22, 32, 36

**G**

gold prospecting, 26
Great Lakes, 8, 10, 11, 26

**H**

*Historical and descriptive account of British America, An*, 32
horses, 16, 17, 18, 19, 22, 23, 29
Hudson Bay, 8, 11, 14
Hudson's Bay Company, 9, 32, 37
Huron, 9, 10

**I**

Inuit, 6, 8
Iroquois, 10, 11

**K**

Kane, Paul, 23–24
Kentucky, 10
Kentucky rifle, 31, 32
Klondike Gold Rush, 37
Kutchin, 42

**L**

Loon Lake, 32

**M**

magic, 14
massacres, 6, 32
matchlock arquebus, features of, 26–27
Métis, 8, 31, 32
Montagnais, 8, 9
Murdoch, John, 40–41
Murray, Hugh, 32

**N**

Naskapi, 8
Nipissing, 8
Northern tribes, how they are geographically defined, 8
Nunivak, 43

**O**

Ohio Valley, 10
Ojibway, 8, 32
Ontario, Lake, 11
Ottawa River, 10

**P**

Piegan, 25
Plains Indians, 6, 7

**Q**

Quebec, 9, 32

**R**

raiding parties, 13, 14, 18, 19, 22–24, 42
Riel, Louis, 31, 32
Riel's Rebellions, 31, 32, 34
rifles, types of, 29–31
Russians, 9, 35

## S

Sampson, Ezra, 5–6
scalping, 18, 22, 24, 25
Seven Years' War, 11, 32
shields, 21, 23, 25, 27, 42
Shoshone, 25
Sioux, 21, 26
smallpox, 24
snowshoes, 14, 19, 36
spears, 41–42
St. Charles, 34
St. Ignace, 10
St. Louis, 10
Stone Age, 8

## T

tipis, construction methods and materials, 13, 15
*Travels to the Source of the Missouri River*, 21–22
tribal palisades, 14

## W

warfare, Native American methods of, 6, 7, 42–43
war lodges, 19, 21–22
War of 1812, 13
war paint, 20, 22
weapons, types of, 25–29, 31, 38–42
woodland tribes, 7

## Y

Yellowknife, 8
*Youth's Companion, The*, 5–6